TELL THE OTHER SIDE OF THE STORY:

EVALUATING & ATTACKING A DOMESTIC VIOLENCE CASE

AF885396

Mark L. Deniz, Esq.

Copyright © 2022 by Mark L. Deniz, Esq.

All rights reserved. No part of this publication may be reproduced, distributed, or transmitted in any form or by any means, including photocopying, recording, or other electronic or mechanical methods, without the prior written permission of the publisher, except in the case of brief quotations embodied in critical reviews and certain other noncommercial uses permitted by copyright law. For permission requests, write to the publisher, addressed "Attention: Permissions Coordinator," at the address below.

Jacobs & Whitehall
21750 Hardy Oak Blvd
Suite 104
#51700
San Antonio, Texas 78258
www.jacobsandwhitehall.com

Ordering Information:

Quantity sales. Special discounts are available on quantity purchases by corporations, associations, and others. For details, contact the publisher at the address above.

Orders by U.S. trade bookstores and wholesalers. Please contact Jacobs & Whitehall: Tel: (888) 991-2766 or visit www.jacobsandwhitehall.com.

Printed in the United States of America

Published in 2022

ISBN: 978-1-954506-32-9

PREFACE

When the police come into your home and arrest you on domestic violence charges without even getting your side of the story, it is incredibly unfair. You want to find solutions to get the best possible outcome in such unfair situations. Many domestic violence charges can be dismissed or reduced before they even reach court. Therefore, you can challenge the government's evidence and take steps such as preparing character and mitigation packets to build your case. To do so, you will want to read about the field of domestic violence and Premier Domestic Violence Law Group's proven and proactive approach. Our success in doing this can be seen in the results, client reviews, testimonials, and awards our firm has obtained.

DEDICATION

To my wife Stacey, who has given my ship a course and direction. To my children, who remind me why I get up and out the door in the mornings. To my dad, who showed me what hard work was. The biggest shout-out is to my mom, Annie Deniz, who passed away as I was writing this book. She always believed in me. She loved me more than anyone else. So much of my soul is because of her. I miss her so much. She had Alzheimer's, which made saying goodbye different than a sudden event.

Our mother/son song was "I Hope You Dance" recorded by Lee Ann Womack. I try every day to get on life's floor and dance. I know she is up in the stars dancing herself and sending her energy to the family.

I love and miss you, mom.

"I love you forever

I like you for always,

As long as I'm living

My [mommy] you'll be."

Robert Munsch, Love You Forever

Disclaimer

This publication is intended to be used for educational purposes only. No legal advice is being given, and no attorney-client relationship is intended to be created by reading this material. The author assumes no liability for any errors or omissions or for how this book or its contents are used or interpreted, or for any consequences resulting directly or indirectly from the use of this book. For legal or any other advice, please consult an experienced attorney or the appropriate expert, who is aware of the specific facts of your case and is knowledgeable in the law in your jurisdiction.

Law Offices of Mark Deniz, APLC
San Diego Office
2831 Camino Del Rio South, Suite 307
San Diego, CA 92108
(858) 429 9982
www.denizdefense.com

TESTIMONIALS

"Mark Deniz did an exceptional job on my case. I had a DV case and was initially charge with a Felony. I was FREAKING out as I have never been charged with a crime. I knew I had to get an attorney because honestly I felt I was innocent of all the charges and if convicted my life would be wrecked. I found Mark off some website and immediately called him. He set up a free 30 min consultation in which I explained my case to him and he offered solutions on how he could help. He broke down the cost in increments, (the package submitted before charges are placed against you, the pretrial and trial.) We never got to the pretrial or trial because he was able to have the DA not press charges against me. I feel extremely satisfied with how Mark handle my case so far. Best of all he didn't charge a ridiculous price, it was fair and well worth it. Thanks Mark for doing an awesome job on my behalf."

– Michelle, Domestic Violence Client

****

"I did not want to go with the public defender. I interviewed several lawyers about my situation. Mr. Deniz worked with me on the finances so I could afford a private attorney. I was able to get out of a situation where I could have been in trouble."

– Nick, Former Client

****

"I thought I was in trouble and was heading into jail for a week or two at least. I did not want to lose my job or be away from the kids. He came in and took control of the situation. I felt the case was always being looked on and there was constant progress. I was glad to be his client and was able to get this behind me. He worked with me on payments. I felt very satisfied and would refer him to other people if they get in a jam."

– Anonymous, Former Client

****

"I was lucky to find Mark. I was scared about losing my job from this. Mark resolved the matter without me losing my job or too much skin off my back. He always communicated with me and let me know I was a priority. I hope never to be in a bind again, but if I am I am calling him."

– Anonymous, Former Client

****

TABLE OF CONTENTS

About The Author

I have focused exclusively on criminal defense since I was sworn in as an attorney in 2003. I spent almost ten years of that time as a prosecutor, and I won many awards during my tenure. I handled thousands of cases from the most basic misdemeanors to three strikes, and twenty-five to life cases. Part of that time was as a domestic violence prosecutor in the Family Protection Unit.

When I moved to the defense side of the aisle, one of the main emphases of my law firm became domestic violence matters. Our goal at Premier Domestic Violence Law Group is to use our experience to forge a proven approach that provides the best possible outcome for our clients.

Domestic violence cases differ from most other criminal defense situations because they often involve two different accounts of what happened. There is the accused's story and that of an alleged "victim." Finding, exonerating, and showing independent evidence plays a major factor in making someone's side of the story heard. An approach exists to unearth the evidence to strengthen the defense's case and illuminate the weaknesses in the government's case.

This eBook provides a glimpse of our law firm's proven and proactive approach, which is forged by experience. This method is taught to other attorneys who are learning about domestic violence. The stakes are high in domestic violence cases, and the consequences are evident. Finding solutions to get the best possible outcome is the key.

Why Have I Written This eBook?

This eBook provides information on the subject of domestic violence criminal defense. It demonstrates that there are solutions and ways to get the best possible outcome after being charged with domestic violence (DV). Often, I see clients like you who have gotten arrested for DV charges, and they often feel what happened doesn't warrant charges or the punishment that they are facing.

After you were arrested and, after getting out on bail, you might start researching the charges you were arrested on. Often there is a disconnect between the situation that you went through and the charges that have been brought against you. In the following, I share a few testimonies of such experiences from people who feel the same way and are realizing that their story was not fully heard. You might feel that everything is closing in on you and that you need help. Premier Domestic Violence Law Group is here to help, and we offer you solutions to get the best possible outcome.

Facts About Domestic Violence (DV)

In most situations, the people who are arrested for domestic violence (DV) have never dealt with the criminal system before. These people span the spectrum of our society. They are 18 to 79 years old, and they are of all economic statuses and ethnicities. Why? Because domestic violence is a sign of issues that are at the root of people's lives, in the form of interpersonal relationships, love, insecurity, handling stress, etc. Many DV situations stem from the tensions of being in a relationship that almost every person experiences. Couples argue and fight. It is a normal part of most relationships, and such tensions can sometimes be difficult to handle.

When does fighting in a relationship crosses over the line to a point where it can get someone in trouble? It is not as far as one would think. It can take place during a worse-than-normal argument. One partner decides to contact the police to make a point to the other. Each partner has crossed the lines of the normal relationship argument parameters. The partner calling 911 does not realize the beast they are unleashing when they call the police. They're unleashing a monster, and they can't take it back once they make that call.

When a partner calls the police, many think, "I'm going to get you back," and "You are going to be kicked out of the house for the night." Or something like, "The cops are going to come and yell at you." In reality, the police are more likely to come and arrest someone.

Partners make this mistake all the time. What they unsuspectedly did is trigger a DV investigation. One that by law leads to an arrest. More importantly, it sends the actors in the fight down a perilous road that has many unintended consequences for both parties. This is the time people should seek out professionals who have the tools to unearth solutions.

CHAPTER 1

CALIFORNIA DOMESTIC VIOLENCE CHARGES DEFINED

When people think of domestic violence (DV), they often think of physical violence when one partner exerts dominance over the other. However, domestic violence crimes include many different actions if it is involved and within a relationship. Many crimes that are prosecuted under the domestic violence statutes may never involve someone touching the other person.

Let us begin with some common DV crimes and scenarios that could potentially result in being arrested on DV charges.

Domestic Violence Or Battery On A Spouse Or A Significant Other

Domestic violence (DV) is defined as a pattern or action of abusive behavior in any relationship that is used by one partner to gain or maintain control over a partner. In most scenarios, actual DV charges that lead to an arrest require some evidence of physical touching and/or a visible injury. However, the prosecution will investigate to determine if there is any prior physical, emotional, or mental abuse to strengthen their case.

Intimidating Or Dissuading A Witness. Witness intimidation is covered under California Penal Code 136.1. It is a crime in California to prevent a victim or witness knowingly and maliciously from providing evidence to law enforcement. By law, it makes no difference if a defendant was successful in preventing a testimony. This is a very common

Domestic violence related charge. Dissuading a witness begins when a couple is arguing. One partner tells the other they are calling the police. The alleged aggressor then grabs the phone and hangs up a phone or takes away their partner's cell phone saying, "Let's not be dumb. Don't call anyone.

Let's talk and work this out." That action can initiate an arrest and can be construed as dissuading a witness.

False Imprisonment. California Penal Code 236 PC describes the crime of false imprisonment as unlawfully depriving another person of their liberty. Put simply, it's a crime to detain, restrain, or confine someone without their consent and not allow them to leave when they want. False imprisonment could be claimed when someone says, "Don't call your mom to come to pick you up," or "Sit here and talk with me," or you prevent them from leaving because you don't want to go to bed angry. You could say, "Let's talk" after a big fight, and put your hand on the door to prevent a wife, girlfriend, or significant other from going to go stay at a friend's house or even their bedroom. That action could be false imprisonment and could lead to an arrest.

Vandalism. California Penal Code 594 PC defines the crime of vandalism as maliciously damaging, destroying, or defacing another person's property. Vandalism is a misdemeanor if the amount of the damage is less than $400 or a felony if $400 or greater. With today's cost of products (especially cell phones), it is very easy to exceed the $400 threshold. If somebody is mad and starts breaking items belonging to both those in the relationship because of a disagreement, this can be vandalism as well.

For example, a wife breaks Christmas gifts that her husband gave to her saying, "These are stupid and meaningless because you treat me like crap." Such actions can be acts of vandalism because those are his items as well. There could be items that are used and belong to her, but because of community property laws, by destroying her things in anger or sadness, she could be committing a crime.

Criminal threats. Penal Code 422 PC defines 'criminal threats' as threats of death or great bodily injury that are intended to place victims in reasonable and sustained fear for their safety or the safety of their families. Such a threat can occur if somebody is making threats to an individual while they are fighting. Someone might be very upset and say, "I'll kill you before you think about taking the kids."

The examples above illustrate how many scenarios can potentially fall under the domestic violence umbrella. Domestic violence crimes can be attached once the prosecution can tie in a relationship between the parties. It can be a first date, a marriage, or an established boyfriend-girlfriend relationship.

A Domestic Violence Arrest Can Happen Quickly

When people call the police to diffuse a situation, they are often surprised to find out that they're the ones who are ultimately arrested for committing a domestic violence crime. The Police often conduct a quick investigation and conclude who is the aggressor and see a scenario that may contain charges of domestic violence or battery, intimidating or dissuading a witness, false imprisonment, vandalism, and criminal threats (described in greater detail above).

When clients come into my office, they discover not only are they charged with domestic violence, but they have also been charged with one of the usual secondary charges that are associated with DV. They learn that domestic violence matters can be charged as both a felony and a misdemeanor. No matter what the police arrest you for, you want to be proactive and begin working for the best possible outcome.

CHAPTER 2

HISTORY OF DOMESTIC VIOLENCE AND ARRESTS

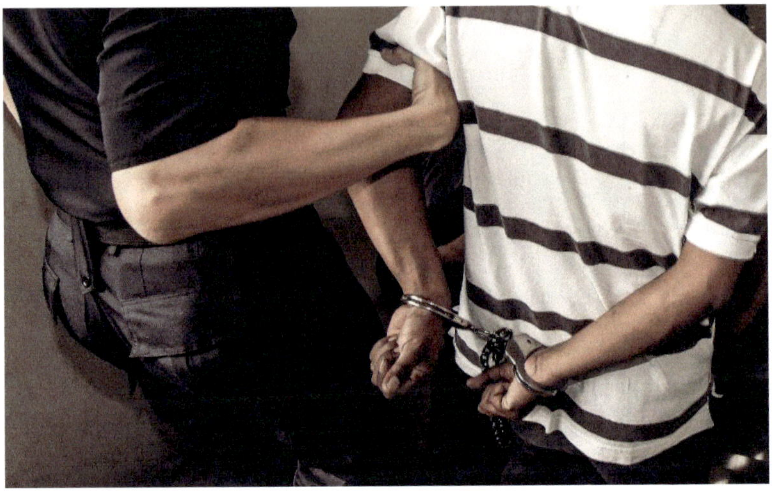

Generally, you will find that an arrest is made at the scene of most all domestic violence (DV) calls. This action was not always the case. Historically, domestic violence has not always been enforced by law enforcement. In fact, for most of history, domestic violence wasn't even considered a crime because women were considered property. In those times, abuse that occurred in the home was accepted.

In the 20th century, there were shifts to be more aware of domestic violence and to curb the behavior. In the 1960s and the 1980s, there were some big pushes to address the issue of DV. As a result, the discretion of police in arresting for domestic violence violations was taken away. They no longer were given the option to make an arrest or not because often there were officers who would feel compassion for the accused aggressors (usually men), who often said they were trying to "lead and take care of their house." The police might get to a scene and the husband says, "My wife flipped out as women do, and I was just trying to hold her." The officers, relating to the person and knowing the consequences of arrest would not make an arrest. The laws changed and led us to today's protocol, which states that any time there was is any evidence of abusive behavior or violence, an arrest shall be made.

People are finding themselves in handcuffs for a situation that might not normally warrant an arrest. The law is almost in a place where the mechanism is to arrest first and deal with the analysis of what happened later. As a response to years of under-enforcement, the pendulum has swung the other way, and there is an over-arrest in these types of cases.

Police Arrival On Scene

When police officers arrive on scene, they conduct a quick investigation. Once they determine the matter is DV related, they often make up their minds quickly on who is the aggressor and who the victim is. Even if the significant other does not want to press charges, the officers are likely to make an arrest.

In the past, when police came to the scene, an officer might have told the accused, "I think you need to leave for tonight." They would leave a warning that they will be arresting someone if they must "come back." That scenario is not happening in modern times. What is happening is the police are mandated to arrest someone, and whether the matter is ultimately prosecuted or not is going to be up to the prosecutors, usually from the District Attorney's Office. This is the new criteria. What happens as a result is a lot of people find themselves being arrested for de minimis (very minimal) actions, where there is mutual blame, and no party wants to press charges.

Independent Evidence

A prosecutor looks for independent evidence when deciding whether to issue charges. Independent evidence is evidence that corroborates or confirms a witness's statements. It is the evidence that "breaks the tie" in most he said/she said scenarios and is important evidence in a DV case. Independent evidence can include (but is not limited to):

- **Injuries.** Police will usually take photos of any injuries of the parties.
- **Witnesses.** These can be persons who observed an incident. They can be neighbors who did not see anything but heard yelling, breaking of items or threats from the suspect, and a 911 call can be independent evidence.
- **Damage.** The police may come and see broken items in the house, car, or other location that can confirm the accounts given by the parties. Independent evidence can often break the tie in he said/she said situations.

People often slam doors or bang objects when they're angry, perhaps breaking something in the process. In situations like this, if the police find out these actions took place and there is evidence to support their assessments, the officers could use these observations to make an arrest.

Prior Incidents

The prosecution may examine a case and determine it is weak. One area that supports their case is to claim there have been prior incidents of domestic violence. The police will ask the alleged victim at the scene whether the accused has been violent before. If the person says no, there is not much for the prosecutor to investigate.

However, in the heat of the moment, people are trying their best to deflect blame. The person talking to the police may believe that she might be the one who will be arrested. So, what does she do? She lays blame on the other person, exaggerating and lying to the police that there have been previous incidents to deflect culpability on her. When the prosecutors see this information in the reports, they begin investigating. There may be previous reports, where the police had to show up.

In most cases, there is no information to support the victim's allegations. Even with no corroboration, the prosecution will purport the accused has a "history" and prior "incidents" of domestic violence. The prosecution will then claim and try to establish a cycle of violence theory, which is a domestic violence theory showing the pattern of abuse (see diagram below).

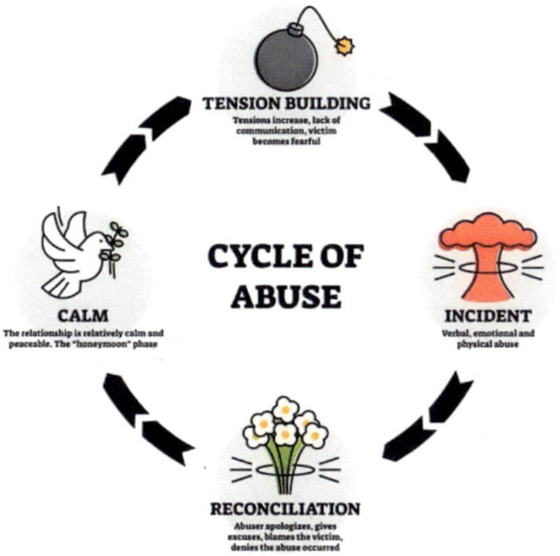

Photo Credit: Soul Shepherding website.
https://www.soulshepherding.org/breaking-free-cycle abuse/

Combating unsubstantiated incidents with facts that show that the cycle of abuse is not part of that relationship dynamic is important. If the accused can establish that prior incidents are unsubstantiated, the cycle of violence theory becomes a weak or nonexistent form of independent evidence. Without independent evidence, it can be difficult for a prosecutor to establish their case.

What Happens After Someone Is Arrested For Domestic Violence Charges

When someone is arrested on domestic violence charges, they are taken into custody and booked into jail. In most cases, these people need to get back home and to work, so they post bail. Once that occurs, the police officers may prepare and file an emergency protective order (temporary restraining order) against that person. The individual who was arrested cannot come within 100 yards of the property or the other person who was part of the incident. That could be devastating for the accused and leaves him vulnerable. This person has been arrested, spent thousands on bail, and it is now illegal for him to go back home. An officer will now have to escort the accused to their house to get any kind of belongings they may need. For a week to ten days, this person will have to stay with family or friends—or at a hotel—while that emergency protective order is in place. It is then up to the prosecution and/or judge to decide if that emergency protective order should be extended.

The intended purpose of the emergency protective order, in theory, is to provide the victim time to pursue a restraining order against an abuser. The victim has around a week to do what she will need to get a restraining order served. The reality is, in many cases, the victim usually does not want any charges filed, and they do not want a restraining order. Even in these cases, it is still illegal for the arrested party to come home while the temporary orders are in effect.

Police officers have varying levels of discretion when it comes to the emergency protective order, which differs from agency to agency. A lot of law enforcement agencies inform their patrol officers to cover themselves and file the emergency protective order in most situations on behalf of the alleged victim. Hypothetically, if the police officer stands down and no order is in place and the accused returns two days later, badly hurting his partner, that officer could find their job in jeopardy. That potential liability often leads officers to say, “I’m going to cover my butt,” so they place the protective order on the accused. It's unfortunate, but understandable why the police officers do that. Domestic violence matters usually result in an arrest of a suspect. Once out of jail, the accused needs to begin repairing his reputation as much as possible before going to court or facing unwarranted consequences.

CHAPTER 3

DETERMINING WHO IS THE AGGRESSOR IN A DOMESTIC VIOLENCE MATTER

Each law enforcement agency has basic domestic violence training that may differ slightly from agency to agency, but generally, an officer is supposed to come on the scene and assess who is the aggressor. They quickly decide who is wearing the black hat (the bad guy) and who is wearing the white hat (the good guy). Unfortunately, the reality is that often the people involved are both wearing gray hats, and both had a hand in the incident. Both crossed lines and neither did anything more than the other. However, grey does not work for police. Their job is to label people "aggressor" or "victim".

Demeanor May Decide Who Is The Aggressor

When the police come to a scene, they're going to interview both individuals. They usually separate the parties and begin talking to them. Sometimes, the police make very quick assumptions about who is going to be the victim and who is going to be the aggressor. They often based this decision on someone's demeanor. When the police arrive, someone might be more angry or uncooperative with the police because they are very emotional. It is found out later that the more cooperative person is the aggressor, and they caused most of the situation. At the scene, police do not dig too deep to find out that fact. When the officers investigate the scene, the reality is the calmer person usually feels guilty, retracting after realizing she's driving against traffic. However, the police conclude that this person is the alleged victim and arrest the other person.

A common scenario is where a husband says something very mean to his significant other. He knows he shouldn't have said what he said to them. He knows it crossed the line. As a result of the statement, the significant other ends up very emotional. When the husband tries to apologize, they push him away, scratching him in the process. When the police arrive on the scene, the significant other is screaming and emotional. The police see the calm husband with scratches and conclude he is the victim. That significant other could end up being arrested because the officers are making assumptions based on a brief investigation without diving into the full context of what happened.

Contact With The Other Party After A Domestic Violence Arrest

As the accused, it is not a good idea to have any contact with the other party while your matter is pending. The event caused a lot of emotions for both people. In many cases, some issues are still unresolved. The issues can sometimes flare back up. When I talk to my clients, I tell them to stay away for a little while to provide some cooling-off time. It doesn't matter if that person wants to help them. There needs to be a period where they are just focusing on themselves and the seriousness of the situation.

After an arrest, an accused might call the other party to ask for help in getting him out of jail, maybe because he didn't get a chance to get his wallet. In many instances, the other party is the only person the accused can call to get help. However, making that call could be violating an emergency protective order if an accused has been served an order. If law enforcement or the prosecution finds out you made the call, you could be charged with a separate charge of violating the emergency protective order. If there is no protective order, then people may still have unresolved issues on top of this arrest. The situation may flare up and result in another call to police.

It is very dangerous for an accused to contact the other party. There are other times when the other party tries to get the accused in even more trouble by baiting the accused to contact them. The communication may seem almost like blackmail. The other party may be saying to the accused to contact her if they wants their help. Otherwise, they will talk to the police. The accused may engage in that conversation, but the person on the other side, the victim, is just doing this to get him in trouble. Every situation is different, and you cannot know the mindset of that individual, who may be feeling hurt, wounded, and angry.

The Impact Of The Other Party (aka Victim) Dropping Charges

A common misconception is if an alleged victim recants domestic violence allegations that the charges will be dropped. In the old days, that was the case and the victim got to decide whether to prosecute or not. However, the logic now is that if that person is in an abusive relationship, they are not able to make a rational decision because of pressure, previous abuse, or potential future threats of abuse. The other party may get pressure not only from the accused but from family, friends, and even society. People will call a victim saying, "What are the kids going to do if the accused loses his job?" Or "Do you want to ruin their life?" This pressure can lead to victims to dropping the charges, even when they don't want to.

For these reasons, the government took the decision-making process away from “victims”. So, does the victim wanting to drop charges carry any weight with the government? It can. The prosecution will take into consideration their opinion when taking in the totality of the evidence and situation. It can carry more weight when it is part of a comprehensive defense.

Chapter 4

Getting Domestic Violence Charges Dismissed Before Court

I am a firm believer in being proactive and encouraging clients to seek out ways to individually grow after a domestic violence (DV) incident. By acting quickly to get an experienced, capable lawyer on your side, many DV charges can be dismissed before they even reach a court. With getting the ball rolling early in the process, you can have the time to challenge the government's evidence and take steps such as preparing mitigation packets to build your case for dismissal or a reduced charge. Our success in implementing a successful approach can be seen in the many positive reviews, testimonials, and awards our attorneys have received.

Our firm focuses on three distinct areas when developing a legal strategy for a defense:

- **Showing Character.** The first step is separating an accused from other defendants. Unfortunately, the Public Defender's office does not meet with its clients before being appointed. Furthermore, many private defense attorneys focus primarily on the facts of the case and evidence. As a former domestic violence prosecutor, establishing a good character for the accused is vital to get the best possible outcome. You want to show the accused has good character, is trusted by people, and is an asset to the community.
- **Finding Legal Issues And Calling Out all Weakness present in the prosecution's Case.**

Examining and scrutinizing the prosecution's case is the most important area to focus on. It is the base of a comprehensive defense. Knowing the subject matter is crucial to finding what you are looking for in terms of evidence. What is not present in the prosecution's facts is as important as what they possess. That is why it is key to retain an attorney who has the approach, experience, and success with domestic violence cases. You want to highlight for the prosecution the proof issues in a case. If the prosecution cannot prove their case, they will be motivated to resolve the matter that ends with the accused winning.

- **Being Proactive.** When someone is arrested on DV charges, they quickly realize how much punishment they may be exposed to. As their case evolves, the case begins to fall within a certain area on the spectrum of best- and worst case scenarios. Once a case starts forming its framework, you want to be proactive. You can utilize this opportunity to get started on tasks that can help bring a favorable resolution. Proactive tasks can include: taking classes, seeking counseling, volunteering at a nonprofit, etc.

Premier Domestic Violence Law Group is dedicated to always being proactive. In many cases, some unhealthy acts/traits/decisions came out and created actions that led to the arrest. The accused could have said the wrong things that he knew were going to inflame the situation. What was said might not have been criminal, but the words took the event to a whole another level. I often tell my clients, there's a difference between doing something wrong and committing a criminal act. An accused should want to take the opportunity to make themself and their relationship better. What someone does not want to do is claim they did nothing wrong, declare themselves as a victim, and roll out blame on other people.

If there was anger, and your actions were unhealthy, then you should start taking anger management courses. Maybe there is an alcohol problem that negatively affects the relationship. Perhaps existing mental health issues cause anxiety or post-traumatic stress disorder (PTSD) that strains the relationship. In San Diego County, we have a large military contingent. Many active military and veterans are dealing with these issues that stem from their service. In these matters, someone can work with providers and the Veterans Affairs Department (VA) to get help. Premier Domestic Violence Law Group often crafts a resolution that has treatment as part of a favorable outcome, which in many cases ends in a dismissal.

Another option is counseling, which can be an invaluable tool. After the accused can find help for personal issues, we usually recommend seeking relationship counseling, especially if they are staying in the relationship. However, we do not recommend that start with couples counseling. The accused should first start with personal counseling. They then can pivot to tackling relationship issues after some time.

An Arrest Can Be A Wakeup Call

When a prosecutor is deciding whether to file charges or not, we want to confidently say, "This has been a wake-up call, and I will not return to a 'back to business as usual' mentality." The prosecutors want to be assured that this isn't going to be a vicious cycle or happen again in this or a new relationship.

People often swear they're never going to get into a DV situation again, and things seem to get better for a time. However, bad habits come back and issues start reappearing. DV is often a cycle, going from one phase to another. The cycle of violence is real. We encourage our clients to be proactive and say, "I've got to break that wheel."

Chapter 5

Domestic Violence Defense Strategy

In building a potential defense strategy in a domestic violence case, it is vital to gather evidence about the relationship. The evidence provides context about the event and the relationship dynamic. It may shed light on why the event happened. A big fight may have been a long time in coming. Consider the following questions: Is somebody in the relationship jealous? Has there been tension for some time? Is somebody being vindictive because of a situation? Are there false allegations being made because of infidelity? Is the couple on the way to being separated or divorced? Are allegations a ploy to gain leverage in a custody battle? The best defenses are often hidden within the facts, and these questions help identify the facts.

Digging Into The Relationship

When we at Premier Domestic Violence Law Group conduct our initial intake with a client, we want to find out the deeper story about the relationship. Domestic violence cases are very factual, and the backstory can start the ignition for what occurred on the date of the incident. Bringing up facts like, "He cheated on her, and she found out," or "She's posting this on Instagram, and now she's saying he did this," are defenses we can bring to the attention of the prosecutor. Such statements can establish or destroy the credibility of a witness. We bring facts that give rise to the prosecutor to look more closely at the victim's actions because it may show the statements are false allegations. Because very few relationships end amicably, many people save face by making up facts to justify the breakup.

Self-Defense In A Domestic Violence Case

One of the main defenses used in DV cases is self-defense, which is part of many DV fact patterns. An accuser's physical actions can be defensive. For example, a boyfriend may brush off the shoulder of his girlfriend. The boyfriend admits he held her, but only because she was hitting him first. The boyfriend may be holding her, telling her to stop hitting him and chill out. This explanation may compromise the government's case. Self-defense should be examined in every DV arrest.

Eliminating Accusations Of Violence And/Or Abuse

The prosecution will want to establish the accused has committed various types of violence that have abused the alleged victim. The prosecution will utilize what is referred to as the Power And Control Wheel (See Figured 2.) The wheel shows the different types of violence and abuse that can occur in relationships. Combatting this theory early in the case is important. The accused attorney will want to collect information and evidence contrary to any alleged abuse or violence. Tackling these issues before any material part of the case is critical. Otherwise, they can hinder the best possible outcome for the accused.

Figure 2: The Power and Control Wheel

Copyright by the Domestic Abuse Intervention Project 202 East Superior Street, Duluth, MN, 55802 218-722-2781

Plea Offer Or Trial In A Domestic Violence Case

In deciding if a case should go to trial or if a client should contemplate taking a plea agreement, the biggest factor to consider is the strength of the government's case. When you break down all of the evidence, it is vital to determine whether the prosecution can prove their case beyond a reasonable doubt.

- **Optics.** The next factor to consider is optics. How is the jury going to view the overall series of events? Juries tend to place themselves in the shoes of the individuals. When they hear the facts they're asking, "Would I have done that?" or "What would I have done in that situation?"

Jurors will think about the details from their perspective. "If I am just holding her there, telling her to settle down, and I didn't hit her . . . I didn't cause violence . . . What is someone supposed to do?" The optics in a scenario like this is favorable for the defense. Conversely, if an accused stepped over the bounds in a situation, perhaps doing things during the event that a juror would say, "I would never do that," then the optics look bad. An example would be being abusive to a puppy during an argument. The accused may have said things that crossed the solid double lines and are even a speed trap. A scenario like this would not be good to present to the jury. I would consider this scenario. For the jury, optics play a strong part in the strength of a domestic violence case.

CHAPTER 6

CONSEQUENCES OF A DOMESTIC VIOLENCE CONVICTION

The consequences of a domestic violence charge are far-reaching. Domestic violence matters can be charged as a felony or a misdemeanor. With most domestic violence cases, there is a distinct possibility of jail time.

A very common item of most DV cases is participation in a Domestic Violence Rehabilitation

Program, also called DVRP. It often is a year-long program, meeting once a week, to teach how to identify abuse and to learn communication tools and techniques. They have different levels of DVRP, for instance, if substance abuse or alcohol is involved and needs to be addressed. There may be an equal emphasis on substance abuse as there is on relationship tools.

A domestic violence conviction comes with many unintended consequences. Beyond jail and education courses, you lose your right to a firearm for the rest of your life. For some people, that could be impactful to their job. Here in San Diego, we deal with many people who are in the military. Losing the right to a firearm can be a career-ending prospect for them.

Additional Consequences Of A Domestic Violence Conviction

When someone is convicted of a domestic violence charge in California, they are usually served a protective or restraining order. This could happen as part of a plea agreement or if they are convicted at a jury trial. A protective order may be served on an accused as soon as the first court date. Someone could find himself with a three-year protective order. This potentially means someone can't go to see their children, home, or significant other for years.

Part of a comprehensive domestic violence defense must address defending the accused from protective orders. One effective tool for this is obtaining a declaration from the alleged victim. You also want that person to go into court to speak to the judge. The declaration should be simple and address the issue the judge is facing by answering the following questions:

1. Does the alleged victim want to press charges?
2. How does the alleged victim respond to the police report?
3. Does the alleged victim feel in danger from the accused?
4. If the alleged victim felt they were in danger, would they call the police?

Figure 3: Declaration

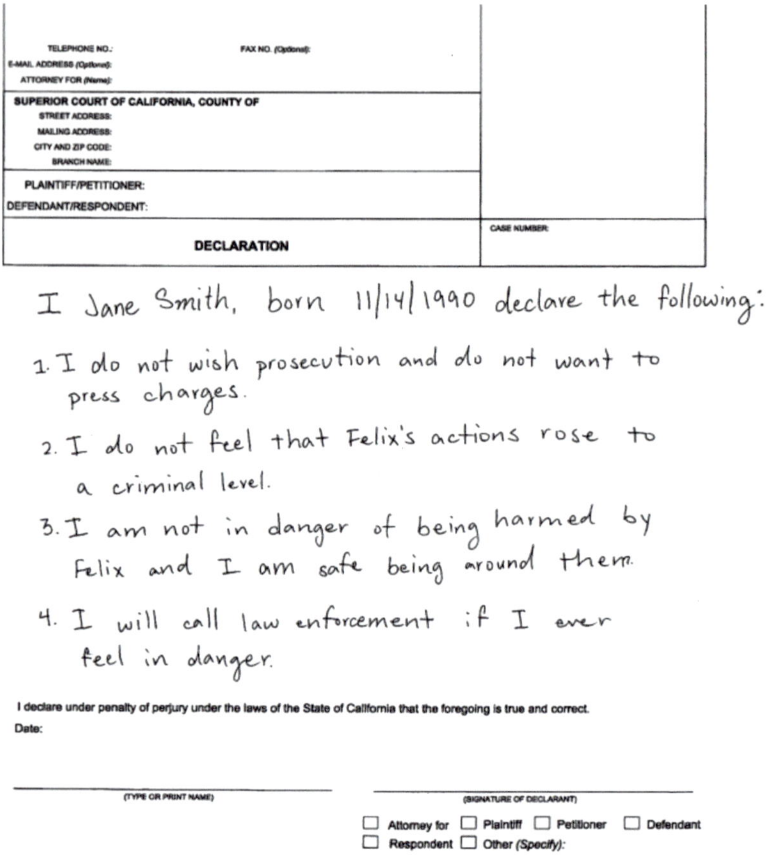

TELEPHONE NO.: FAX NO. (Optional):
E-MAIL ADDRESS (Optional):
ATTORNEY FOR (Name):

SUPERIOR COURT OF CALIFORNIA, COUNTY OF
STREET ADDRESS:
MAILING ADDRESS:
CITY AND ZIP CODE:
BRANCH NAME:

PLAINTIFF/PETITIONER:
DEFENDANT/RESPONDENT:

DECLARATION

CASE NUMBER:

I Jane Smith, born 11/14/1990 declare the following:

1. I do not wish prosecution and do not want to press charges.
2. I do not feel that Felix's actions rose to a criminal level.
3. I am not in danger of being harmed by Felix and I am safe being around them.
4. I will call law enforcement if I ever feel in danger.

I declare under penalty of perjury under the laws of the State of California that the foregoing is true and correct.

Date:

(TYPE OR PRINT NAME) (SIGNATURE OF DECLARANT)

☐ Attorney for ☐ Plaintiff ☐ Petitioner ☐ Defendant
☐ Respondent ☐ Other (Specify):

Source: https://www.courts.ca.gov/documents/mc030.pdf

If a judge issues a protective order, they will often implement a gradual reunification plan or modify an order that puts a protective order in place but is reviewed at a future hearing. If the victim wants to see the other party, they may be able to help lift the order. For example, someone may have a bad alcohol problem, which contributed to the event. The prosecution wants to be satisfied that the alcohol issues are addressed before they allow that individual to go back home.

Domestic Violence Charges And Employment

Part of a domestic violence arrest is dealing with the consequences domestic violence charges may have on your employment. Domestic violence (DV) is a buzz word for employers, who will need to determine whether it is safe to keep you at work. This happens with military service members, firefighters, teachers, police, and other governmental positions. Human Resources (HR) will want to get statements and do investigations before they can let someone back to work. A DV charge can give a potential or current employer, some pause about who you are and how you might deal with people if you get mad at the workplace. HR may determine you are a liability to either hire or keep on. You want to obtain the best possible outcome. Several unintended consequences can occur from a domestic violence arrest.

Domestic Violence and Children

There are situations where Child Protective Services (CPS) gets involved after a domestic violence arrest. Oftentimes children are at the scene of a DV incident. For CPS to get notice of your situation, children do not need to be present in the same room during the dispute. A lot of fighting happens in the parents' bedroom, late at night, when the children are asleep in their bedrooms. Even in these cases, the police will often forward the case to CPS. The prospect (however slight) of having your children taken away is a very scary scenario. If CPS is called, they must substantiate or unsubstantiated an action by conducting an interview.

CPS interviews are something that an accused must be very mindful of because they want to be cooperative with Child Protective Services while keeping as many rights as possible. Some attorneys (with insufficient domestic violence experience) might tell you to not say anything to CPS, which is the golden rule in most criminal cases. The reality is if you do that with CPS, they may deem you uncooperative, which could make you risk losing your children. It is an obstacle-filled road, but in most cases, you must walk the line of adhering to your rights and yet be cooperative with CPS.

Immigration Consequences

Another consequence of a domestic violence (DV) conviction is potential deportation if you are not a U.S. citizen. A domestic violence charge is considered a moral turpitude offense. If you are not a U.S. citizen, your visa can be revoked. In San Diego, we have several students, professionals, and other persons here on visas, green cards, and through other temporary means. Even with a misdemeanor charge, someone can find their visa revoked for a DV event. It is yet another reason to work for the best possible outcome.

CHAPTER 7

BENEFITS OF EFFECTIVE DOMESTIC VIOLENCE ATTORNEY REPRESENTATION

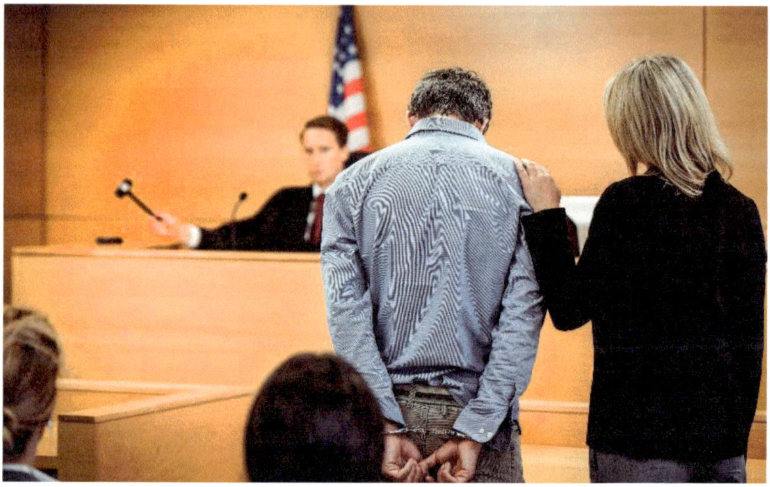

Domestic violence (DV) cases have the highest percentage of dismissal and charges that are not issued than any other type of case in criminal defense. The bar is so low at the arrest stage that little evidence is needed to make an arrest. Fast forward to the issuing phase, where a prosecutor is figuring out whether they can proceed and prove a case beyond a reasonable doubt.

The divide with the elements required at the DV arrest stage and a viable prosecution case is significant. The time between arrest and court is an opportunity for the defense to get their side of the story heard. It is vital to provide the prosecution context before they make their decision of whether to file charges or not. Domestic violence prosecutors are usually specially assigned to cases. These prosecutors are often going to be handling the case from start to finish, so a good approach is to prepare the road early for working the entire case with that prosecutor.

Arguing In Relationships Is Common With Juries

In criminal law cases, the jury often cannot relate one bit to the person who is sitting at that defendant's table. Perhaps they're charged with stealing, elder abuse, or even driving under the influence (DUI). In those cases, most of those people on a jury cannot imagine committing acts even resembling those crimes. This is not the case with domestic violence. When attorneys are explaining to juries about a DV case, the jurors bring up stories that occurred in their own lives that are very similar to the facts at trial. Couples argue and fight. In many cases, regular people have domestic violence-type experiences either in their past or in their current relationships. The result is the jury can put themselves in the shoes of the accused. This common experience is a factor when weighing the totality of the situation in a domestic violence case.

When a prosecutor is looking at the case and considering whether they could be successful in prosecuting a case, they must keep the success they will have with the jury in mind. When I have a client who has good character and he is going to present well in telling their story, it plays well for defense. Attorneys want to work to get to a place where they are confident that there are not going to be 12 people who are going to agree that their client committed a crime. That scenario weighs heavily when the prosecutor has to decide whether to issue charges or not. If I, as an experienced domestic violence attorney, can impress the weakness in their case early in the process, it can put the defense in position to get the best possible outcome.

CHAPTER 8

HOW TO HELP OBTAIN THE BEST POSSIBLE OUTCOME

The most important thing you can do to help your domestic violence defense (DV) case is to share all the necessary information with your attorney. Hold nothing back. The attorney needs to get a sense of the relationship dynamic and what eventually led to the incident. We call this the relationship DNA. That dive into the relationship usually causes an accused to reflect on the relationship. It can get personal, but such reflection is often necessary to explain your side to the prosecution and judge.

The ideal client, working for the best possible outcome, is someone willing to look in the mirror and say, "I need to change." In most DV situations, whether the charges get dismissed or not, there are underlying issues that need to be addressed. Someone needs to be willing to do the work in as positive a manner as possible. As hard as that can be during a case, that effort will be an invaluable help.

When our firm is dealing with clients, we see a lot of their personal shortcomings. Some clients are not ready to put in the work needed to address issues and inevitably it hurts their case. Some people react in different ways to the process. Some people get very defensive and skeptical, believing they did nothing wrong. It can be an emotional time for an accused. Some clients believe the world has wronged them. It is vital to shift that mindset because that kind of thinking can crash a defense. Someone might think the law and everyone else is the problem and not them. One silver lining of a domestic violence incident is it can make you stop and take in what is going on in their life. It provides you with a landmark to make changes.

The Premier Domestic Violence Law Group Difference

What sets Premier Domestic Violence Law Group apart from others is our dedication to letting our client's side of the story be heard. We find out who the prosecutor is as soon as possible. The prosecutor is generally handling the case from the time that it gets on their desk to the time that it gets resolved. Thus, working well with the prosecutor early on is important.

As a former domestic violence (DV) prosecutor, we have a history of working on DV cases in San Diego. We have an approach that is forged from experience. We have a relationship with the prosecutors, which enhances our lines of communication and strengthens our working relationships. There is trust among our counterparts, even though we are opponents.

Next, as the prosecutors decide whether to issue charges, they are considering the strength and experience of the defense attorney. If the accused's lawyer is someone who handles domestic violence cases regularly, knows about the cycle of violence and prosecution theories, and can confidently demonstrate a level of expertise, it gives the prosecutor pause before deciding what to do on a case.

We have frequent working relationships with the prosecution because we focus on domestic violence cases. By talking to the same prosecutor again and again, we build up trust and a working relationship that helps our clients. That may not happen if you are a lawyer in a general practice who takes on cases in multiple areas of criminal defense.

Many domestic violence cases are borderline as to whether the prosecutor is going to file charges or not. Finding a good domestic violence attorney to handle the case at the start can help get the best possible outcome. The right attorney may get charges reduced or dismissed by painting the whole picture for the prosecutor. Thus, we can demonstrate to the prosecution the weakness of their case before the accused walks into court.

What also sets us apart from other DV defense firms is our level of training. First, our firm teaches lawyers on domestic violence. It is seasoned attorneys who attend our trainings to learn a proven approach. I spent almost ten years as a prosecutor, including an assignment with the Domestic Violence Unit. Praised for its unique approach to prosecuting domestic violence cases, this special unit is a state-of-the-art program by the National Council of Juvenile and Family Court Judges. My experience with that unit has helped forge a proven approach, through experience, on how to defend domestic violence cases. Attorneys in the unit hear from speakers, psychologists, and other DV experts, who discuss the field of domestic violence. These lawyers get trained to evaluate domestic violence cases, how to identify abuse, and most importantly, how best to win your case.

Coming from that side, the prosecution structure has helped me over the years to communicate and speak to the DV prosecutors. They are aware that I know what they know. They know I have the experience and knowledge to properly weigh the strength of a case. For example, if the defense can show no abusive history, they know I'm going to communicate that to a jury. This fact increases the chances of giving you the best possible outcome. That's what we work for at Premier Domestic Violence Law Group.

It Is About Finding SOLUTIONS

A lot of attorneys can identify the problems in a case. The harder question to answer is finding solutions. You, as the client, may want to know, "How am I going to get out of this?" or "How am I going to stay out of jail?" Those are the questions that you want a lawyer for. It's not to just tell you what can go wrong or give the worst-case scenario. Your lawyer's efforts are on getting you the best possible outcome. That's what we at Premier Domestic Violence Law Group focus on.

Conclusion

It is incredibly unfair when the police come into your home and arrest you on domestic violence charges without even getting your side of the story. At Premier Domestic Violence Law Group, we begin by listening to your side. Our experienced San Diego based DV defense attorneys will do everything in their power to tell your story, protect your rights, and get you the best possible outcome.

We are all about **solutions.**

INDEX

NOTES

Made in the USA
Monee, IL
05 November 2026

67387950R00043